LET'S FIND OUT ABOUT

FALL

by

MARTHA and CHARLES SHAPP

Pictures by László Roth

GROLIER INTERNATIONAL INC.

575 Lexington Avenue, New York 22

Authorized reprint of an edition
published by Franklin Watts, Inc.

Library of Congress Catalog Card Number: 62-13950

There are four seasons in the year —

winter,

spring,

summer,

and fall.

Some people like winter best.

Some people like spring.

Some like summer.

Others like fall best of all.

When is fall?

Fall is when you are back in school after summer vacation.

Fall is when it gets cool.

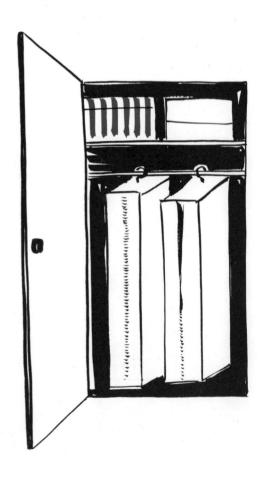

You put away summer clothes and put on warmer clothes.

In the fall the days get shorter and shorter.
You can't play outdoors very long after school.

It gets dark too early.

The sudden frost that comes on a fall night kills many flowers.

One day the flowers are tall and bright.

The next day the flowers are dead.

The leaves of many trees change color in the fall.

In the fall many animals get ready for winter.

The fur on some animals gets thicker.

Some animals put away food for the winter.

Many birds fly away to warmer places.

The frogs go down to the bottom of the pond.

There they sleep all winter.

In the fall the caterpillar makes a cocoon in which it sleeps all winter.
While it sleeps, the caterpillar changes into a moth.

In the spring the moth comes out of the cocoon.

People get ready for winter, too.

Vegetables are picked and put away for winter food.

Fruit is picked for winter food.

Halloween comes in the fall.

Thanksgiving Day comes in the fall.
The first Thanksgiving dinner was long ago.

37

Thanksgiving Day is still celebrated every fall

with a Thanksgiving dinner.

There are four seasons in the year,

winter,

spring,

summer,

fall.

Which season is the best season of all?

VOCABULARY (100 words)

a
after
ago
all
and
animals
are
away

back
best
birds
bottom
bright

can't
caterpillar
celebrated
change(s)
clothes
cocoon
color
comes
cool

dark
day(s)
dead
dinner
down

early
every

fall
first
flowers
fly
food
for

four
frogs
frost
fruit
fur

get(s)
go

Halloween

in
into
is
it

kills

leaves
like
long

makes
many
moth

next
night

of
on
one
others
out
outdoors

people
picked
places
play

pond
put

ready

school
season(s)
shorter
sleep(s)
some
spring
still
sudden
summer

tall
Thanksgiving
that
the
there
they
thicker
to
too
trees

vacation
vegetables
very

warm(er)
was
when
which
while
winter
with

year
you